HABITATS

By
William Anthony

BookLife
PUBLISHING

©2019
BookLife Publishing Ltd.
King's Lynn
Norfolk PE30 4LS

A catalogue record for this book is available from the British Library.

ISBN: 978-1-78637-852-1

Written by:
William Anthony

Edited by:
Madeline Tyler

Designed by:
Gareth Liddington

Photocredits:

4 - Rvector, Lio putra, 5 - Beskova Ekaterina, practicuum, Tarikdiz, AnnstasAg, Tartila, 6 - Kirasolly, 8 - artbesouro, Molesko Studio, 9 - Hennadii H, 10 - KatePilko, Taras Dubov, 11 - NPavelN, 12 - Natali Snailcat, 13 - MrVettore, 14 - Andrei YUL, Spreadthesign, 15 - Giuseppe_R, 16 - Tarikdiz, Rhoeo, 17 - brgfx, lukpedclub, BSVIT, paradesign, 18 - Jemastock, NotionPic, 19 - A7880S, 20 - mainfu, 21 - Hanaha, Incomible, 22 - Oliver Hoffmann, Tarikdiz,

Images are courtesy of Shutterstock.com. With thanks to Getty Images, Thinkstock Photo and iStockphoto.

CONTENTS

Words that look like <u>this</u> can be found in the glossary on page 24.

WHAT ARE HABITATS?

A habitat is a place where something lives. Deserts, mountains and oceans are examples of habitats.

Living things need five main things in their habitats: food, water, shelter, space and enough air.

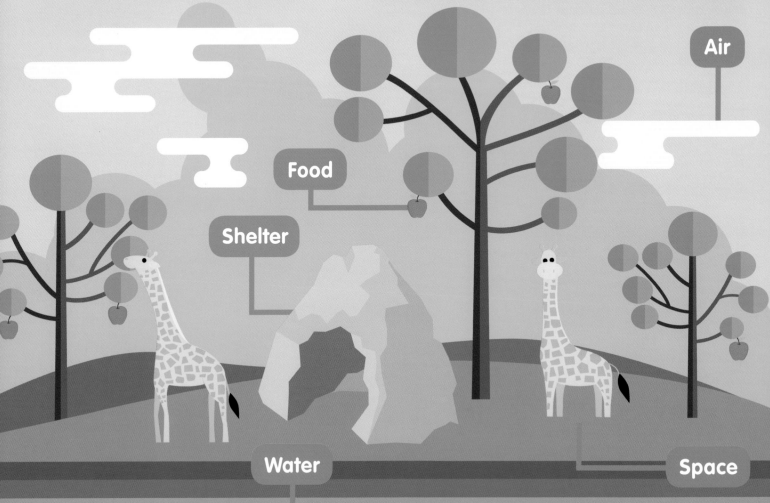

Air

Food

Shelter

Water

Space

Living things have <u>adapted</u> to live in their habitats.

Polar bears live in the cold, snowy Arctic. They have thick fur to keep warm.

African elephants have big ears they can flap. This keeps them cool on hot days in Africa.

Cacti live in dry deserts. They have large stems to store lots of water.

RAINFORESTS

Rainforests are full of lots of tall trees and incredible animals. Tropical rainforests are found near the Equator. Temperate forests are found farther away from the Equator.

Equator

Tropical

Temperate

Rainforests are made up of different layers.

Emergent layer – an area with the highest treetops

Canopy – a sunny area of tall trees

Understorey – a damp, shaded area of short trees

Forest floor – the ground of the rainforest

7

DESERTS

A desert is an area of very dry land with hardly any rain.

40°C

Day

0°C

Night

Some deserts have very <u>extreme temperature</u> changes. They can change from around 40 degrees Celsius in the day to 0 degrees Celsius at night.

Only two and a <u>half</u> centimetres of rain falls in the Sahara in Africa every year.

Desert animals are adapted to live in high temperatures. The Cape ground squirrel has a bushy tail which it uses to make its own shade.

COASTS

Coasts are the areas where the land meets the oceans and seas. There are lots of different types of coast. Some coasts include:

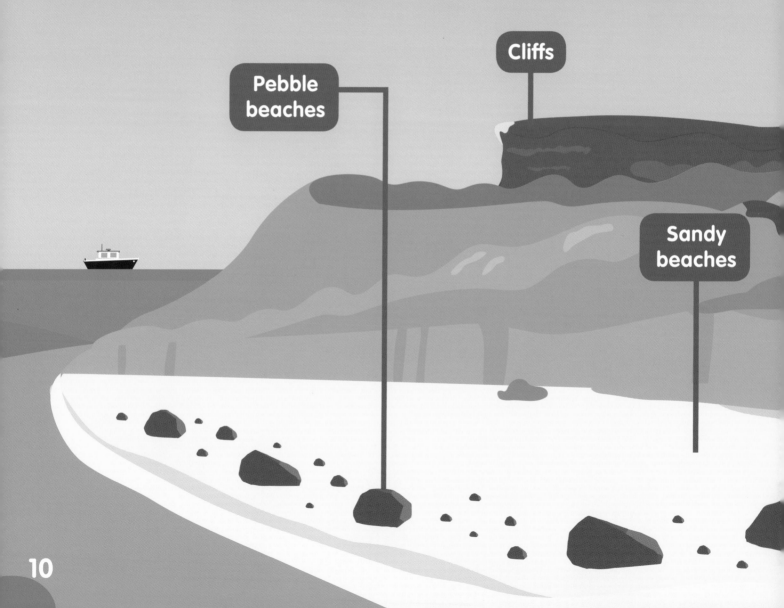

Pebble beaches

Cliffs

Sandy beaches

Lots of animals with shells, such as mussels, are adapted to live on coasts without washing away. They can stick to rocks so well that waves can't pull them off.

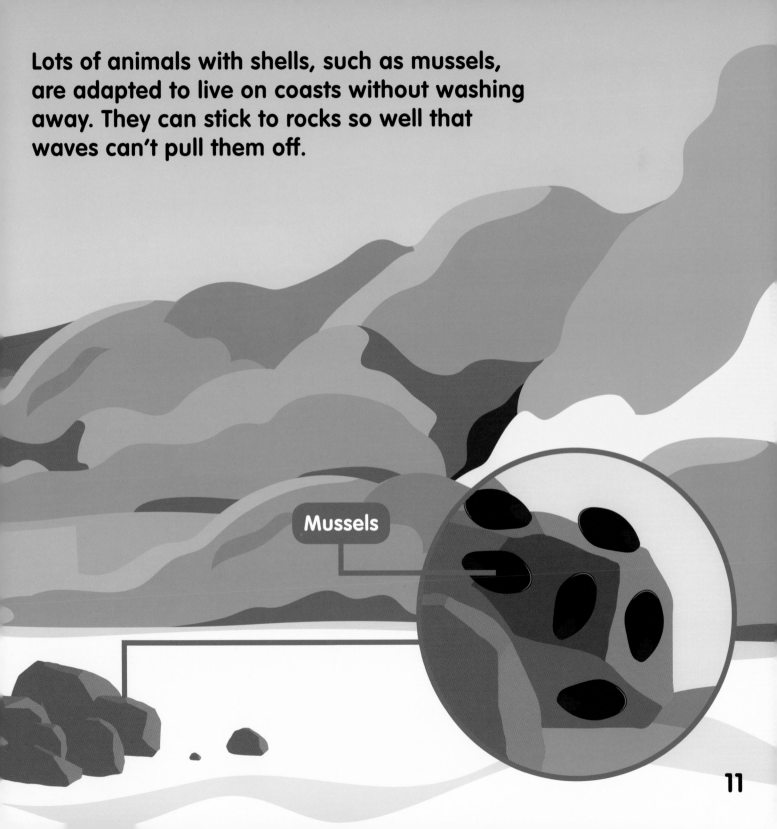

Mussels

OCEANS

Our planet has five huge areas of water, called oceans. We also have lots of smaller areas of water, called seas. The five oceans are:

Arctic Ocean

Pacific Ocean

Atlantic Ocean

Southern Ocean

Indian Ocean

Over seven-tenths of our planet is covered in water.

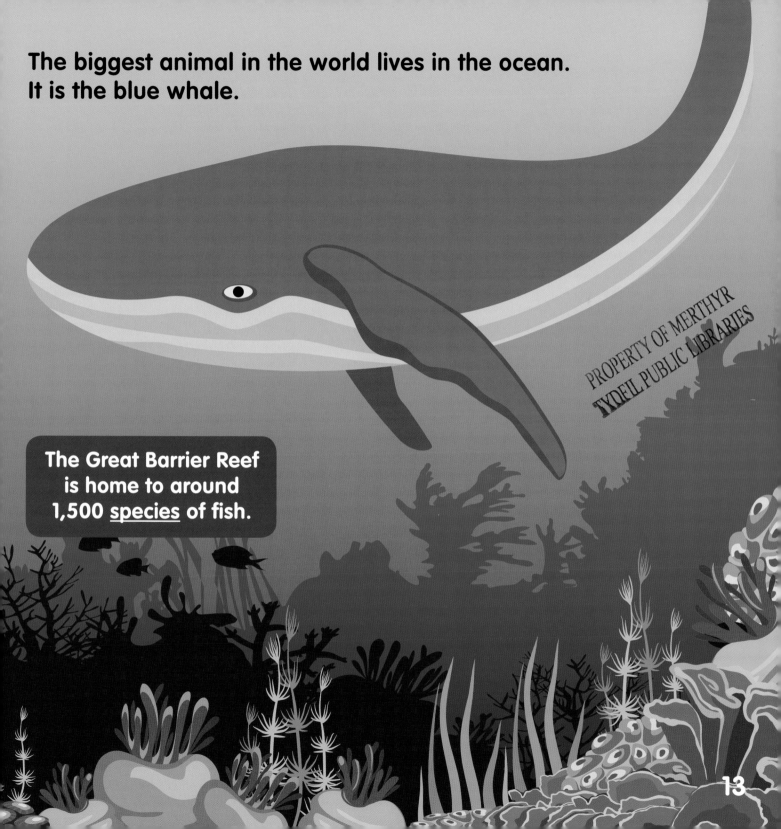

The biggest animal in the world lives in the ocean. It is the blue whale.

The Great Barrier Reef is home to around 1,500 <u>species</u> of fish.

GRASSLANDS

Grasslands are large, open areas of land where lots of different grasses grow. Across the world, they are home to lots of different animals, from wolves to zebras.

Around one-half of Africa is covered in grasslands.

Hiding from <u>predators</u> can be difficult in grasslands. Meerkats use underground burrows to stay out of sight.

15

MOUNTAINS

Mountains are habitats that rise high up towards the sky. They can be very rocky and get very cold near the top.

Not many animals live at the very top of a mountain.

Some plants and animals live halfway up because they are adapted to live in the conditions.

Mountain goat

Beaver

Lots of animals and plants live at the bottom because it is warmer and easier to breathe.

American black bear

17

MICROHABITATS

Some very small animals, such as <u>minibeasts</u>, have their own small habitat inside a bigger one. These are called microhabitats.

Dragonflies live near ponds and lakes. Their <u>offspring</u> live in water until they are fully grown.

Pond

Rock

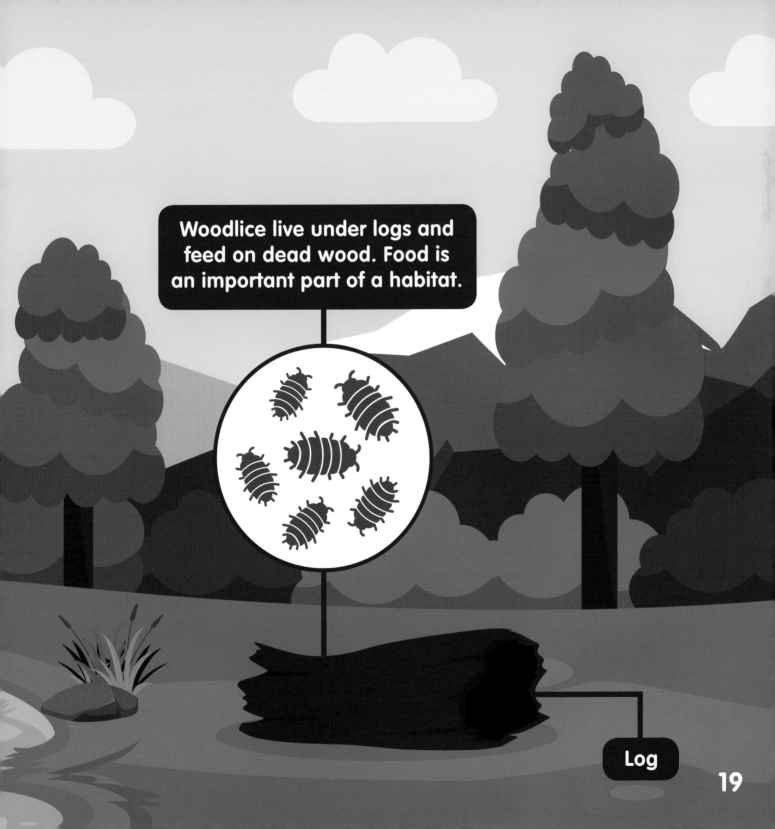

Woodlice live under logs and feed on dead wood. Food is an important part of a habitat.

Log

19

EXTREME ADAPTATIONS

Fish that live in the Arctic Ocean have adapted to stop themselves freezing in the icy water.

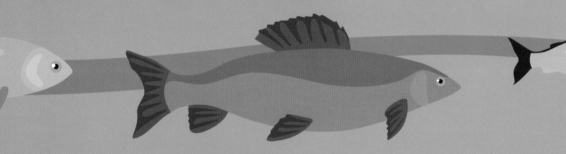

The sword-billed hummingbird has a very long, thin beak to reach inside flowers for food.

The Texas horned lizard can shoot blood from its eyes to scare away predators.

The sperm whale can hold its breath for over an hour so it can dive deep into the ocean for food.

DESTROYING HABITATS

Humans are destroying the habitats of many animals.

By burning lots of coal, oil and gas, we are causing the planet to heat up. This is melting the ice in polar habitats.

Walking or riding a bike is better for our planet than taking the car.

Humans are cutting down trees all over the world. We have destroyed around one-half of the planet's forests during our time on the Earth.

We can reduce the number of trees being cut down by <u>recycling</u> paper.

GLOSSARY

adapted changed over time to suit the environment

conditions the state of the environment, such as the temperature, rainfall and food available

Equator the imaginary line around the Earth that is an equal distance from the North and South Poles

extreme much beyond what is usual or expected

half one of two equal parts of something

minibeasts small animals that do not have an internal skeleton, such as an insect or a spider

offspring the young of an animal or plant

predators animals that hunt other animals for food

recycling using again to make something new

seven-tenths seven of ten equal parts of something

species a group of very similar animals or plants that can create young together

temperature how hot or cold something is

INDEX